You·Can·Draw
FABULOUS
CARTOONS

A DK PUBLISHING BOOK

Project Editor Patricia Grogan
Art Editor Peter Radcliffe
Managing Editor Jane Yorke
US Editors William Lach, Kristin Ward
Senior Art Editor Marcus James
Production Lisa Moss

First American Edition, 1998
2 4 6 8 10 9 7 5 3

Published in the United States by DK Publishing, Inc.
95 Madison Avenue, New York, NY 10016

Visit us on the World Wide Web at
http://www.dk.com

Published in Great Britain by Dorling Kindersley Limited.

ISBN 0-7894-2822-9

Color reproduction by GRB, Italy
Printed in Belgium by Proost

Photography by Andy Crawford, Mike Dunning,
Neil Fletcher, Alan Hills, Dave King, Ray Moller,
Tracy Morgan, and Jerry Young.

DK would like to thank
Almudena Díaz for DTP design, Mark Haygarth for
jacket design, Samantha Gray for editorial assistance,
Penny Lamprell for design assistance, Tom Worsley
for picture research, and Mrs. G. Harwood for allowing
us to reproduce the photograph of her horse,
Wychwood Dynascha.

You·Can·Draw
FABULOUS CARTOONS

Grahame Corbett

Contents

DK PUBLISHING, INC.

Introduction

This book shows you how to improve your cartoon drawings quickly by following a few simple rules. First, consider the proportions of your chosen cartoon subject. Then draw some basic outline shapes, which exaggerate the features you want to emphasize. Finally, sketch in guidelines to help you position the features.

Exaggerating proportion

Before you start, study a photograph of the animal or person you want to draw. Look at the subject's pose, body proportions, and how the body parts align. Use this knowledge to decide which features to exaggerate to comic effect in your cartoon.

The real bear has a small head and pointed, fierce features.

The cartoon bear has a large, round body.

The head is drawn much bigger, and the facial features are enlarged and rounded to add to the friendly expression.

The bear's legs are almost half its total height.

The cartoon bear's legs are shorter and the feet are larger than a real bear's.

The height of this girl's head fits into her total height about seven times.

The head in this cartoon is twice as big as the girl's head in the photograph.

The feet and hands are small in relation to the rest of the body.

The hands look comical when they are made larger than in real life.

The smile is an ideal feature to exaggerate.

The top of the leg is approximately the halfway point on the girl's body.

The size of the girl's feet has been increased and the shoelaces exaggerated.

Using guideline shapes

The outline of your cartoon character is easier to draw if you divide it into a few basic shapes first.

Draw a detailed outline around the shapes.

Guidelines are drawn in blue to help you see them.

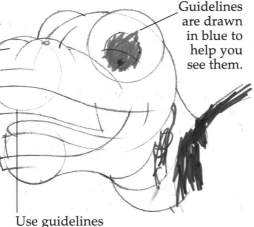

Using photographs

First, use photographs to look for features to exaggerate.

Here, the dinosaur's head and body are the obvious features to accentuate.

Drawing shapes

Start creating your cartoon character by sketching simple shapes to represent your subject's exaggerated proportions.

Sketch large circles and ovals to represent the head and body.

Draw simple lines to represent the legs.

Use guidelines to help you add the features.

Adding features

Finally, draw a more detailed outline around the simple shapes. Sketch in guidelines to position details and the features of your character.

Movement lines

You can bring your cartoon character to life by adding a few simple lines to indicate movement.

Small semicircular lines around the ears indicate flapping movements.

Straight whizz lines close together show the boy is running very quickly.

Light, dotted lines show the arms are moving up and down.

Multiple lines indicate fast-moving legs as the boy sprints along.

Short impact lines show that the kangaroo jumped from this point on the ground.

Long, curved, angled lines suggest a giant leap.

Drawing techniques

Use colored pencils and felt-tipped pens to draw your cartoons.

Use light-colored pencils to draw your outline shapes and guidelines.

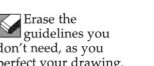 Erase the guidelines you don't need, as you perfect your drawing.

Shade in your cartoons with solid colors.

Use a dark pencil or pen to draw a heavy outline around your finished cartoon.

Cartoon animals can be drawn in just a few simple steps. Whether you draw them from real life or from a photograph the rules are basically the same. Study the animal and emphasize its dominant features. Most importantly, add an expression that brings it to life and makes the cartoon funny.

Standing dog

Follow the steps on this page and transform this beagle into a cartoon. Exaggerate the tail, floppy ears, and big eyes.

Study the angle of the legs and tail before you sketch them in.

The chest and hindquarters form two circles.

1 Draw simple circle guidelines for the position of the body, head, and paws. Add lines for the legs and tail.

Draw a large eye to emphasize the dog's expression.

Erase the guidelines you don't need.

Make the body look stockier than it is in the photograph.

Use a soft pencil to achieve a dark outline.

Leave a glint of white in the eye and nose.

A smile makes the dog look friendly.

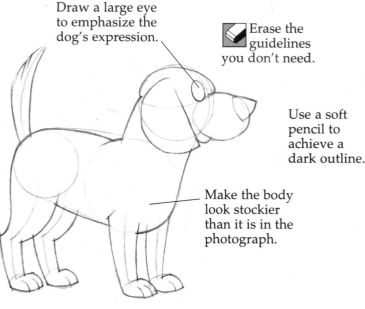

2 Next, draw in the outline of your cartoon dog. Use guidelines to position the ear, nose, and mouth.

3 Finally, color in the dog's coat markings and spend time developing the facial features.

Scratching dog

Now practice drawing your cartoon dog in a different pose, like this scratching dog. As before, start by drawing your basic guidelines. The shapes are the same, just placed differently.

Draw circles for the head, muzzle, and nose.

Add circles to the ends of the leg lines for paws.

Movement lines create a wagging tail effect.

Crossed eyes and raised eyebrows emphasize the dog's irritation.

Add lots of movement lines to animate the legs and paws.

Prowling bear

Now try drawing this big, friendly bear. Study the photograph to get an idea of the most dominant features, which need to be emphasized in your cartoon version.

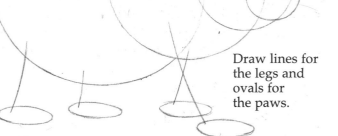

Draw two large circles for the body and shoulders.

Add two smaller circles for the face and muzzle.

Remember to make the eyes bigger to create a friendly face.

Draw lines for the legs and ovals for the paws.

1 Draw the guideline body shapes as shown above, making sure that the legs look shorter than in the photograph.

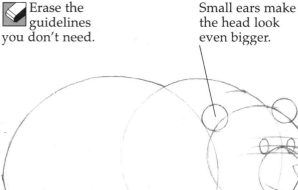

Erase the guidelines you don't need.

Small ears make the head look even bigger.

Draw a small triangle for the nose, and a line for the mouth.

2 Draw in the bear's body outline. Use more guidelines to help you position the ears, eyes, nose, and mouth.

Use a soft colored pencil for the fur effect.

Raised eyebrows and a sideways glance give the bear character.

3 Now, draw the outline in dark pencil and shade in the fur. Color the face in a lighter color so that the features stand out.

Sitting bear

When you have mastered the bear cartoon above, try drawing it in a sitting position. This example has an additional prop, which helps tell a story. The honeycomb and bees liven up the picture and add more character to the bear.

Draw the guidelines and shapes in their new positions.

The dripping honeycomb and bees show that the bear is hungry.

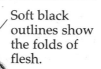

Soft black outlines show the folds of flesh.

Draw the paws more like hands.

Animated animals

Animals move in many different ways. Whether they fly or leap, run or scurry, exaggerating their movements and body shapes adds humor to your cartoons. Look at the examples on these two pages, then try drawing moving animals yourself.

Flying
This purposeful cartoon bird has a large beak and straight movement lines to emphasize its determination.

Draw semicircles for the basic shape of this bird's wings.

Movement lines animate the flapping wings.

Walking
These camel and lion cartoons reflect a proud arrogance in the way they walk. Both animals strut, hold their heads high, and gently flick their tails.

Add movement lines to show the hump is wobbling.

Use shapes to emphasize the knobby knees and large hump.

A large semicircle for the mane takes up most of the body.

Short movement lines indicate the quick flicking of the tails.

Draw the feet at different angles.

The height of the lifted paw exaggerates the prancing motion.

The dragged-back ears give a sense of how fast the kangaroo is moving.

Bounding
The kangaroo's powerful legs and giant feet are exaggerated to show how it moves in leaps and bounds.

Long, sweeping lines show how far the kangaroo has jumped.

The body and muzzle are made up of ovals.

Short, fanned-out lines show where the kangaroo bounced.

Scampering

The monkey's scampering movements are emphasized by exaggerating its long, thin limbs and large hands and feet. The wide eyes and mischievous grin also add a lively feel to the cartoon.

Short movement lines around the joints help indicate twitchy movements.

Draw a short, oval body, with a long, thin tail and limbs.

The wide arms and legs of the monkey's stance indicate its awkward walk.

Leaping

Draw your cartoon frog leaping toward its next meal, stretching everything from the ends of its toes to the tip of its tongue.

The speed and length of the frog's leap is shown by long, sketchy movement lines.

Draw one oval for the body and two circles for the large eyes.

Exaggerate the length of the toes on the end of the frog's long feet.

Running

Notice how this rooster's wings are positioned like a human runner's arms. To show a frantic pace, both feet are off the ground and the neck is craning forward.

Draw a circular body and semicircular wings for the basic guideline shapes.

Lots of closely drawn movement lines and a large cloud of dust show movement at high speed.

Monsters

Monsters make ideal subjects for cartoons because they have such distinctive features. This dinosaur, for example, has a very aggressive facial expression. The unusual body proportions make it easier to work out which features to exaggerate.

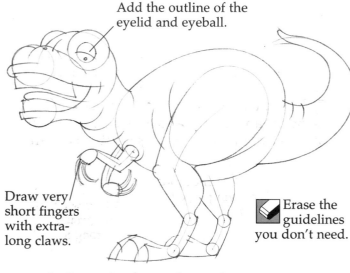

Vicious dinosaur

Follow the steps shown here and transform this roaring *Tyrannosaurus rex* into a monster cartoon.

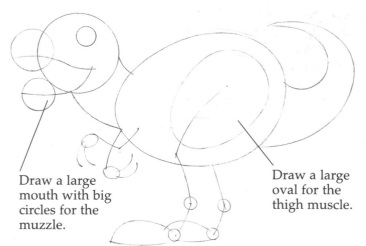

Draw a large mouth with big circles for the muzzle.

Draw a large oval for the thigh muscle.

1 Draw large ovals for the body and a circle for the head. Add lines for the arms, legs, and large tail.

Add the outline of the eyelid and eyeball.

Draw very short fingers with extra-long claws.

Erase the guidelines you don't need.

2 Draw in the outline of your cartoon *Tyrannosaurus rex*. Use guidelines to position the eye, nose, mouth, and fangs.

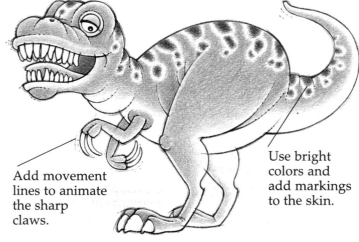

Add movement lines to animate the sharp claws.

Use bright colors and add markings to the skin.

3 Finally, color in the *Tyrannosaurus rex*, adding skin markings and claws. Spend time developing the ferocious expression.

Monster fish

Here you can learn how to transform this colorful fish into an underwater monster.

Use guidelines to position the fin shapes.

Sketch a large, oval body and a large, circular eye.

Draw line details on the fins, and finish in bright colors.

Add two large teeth for a monster effect.

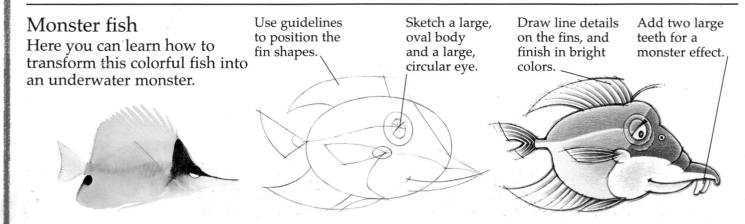

Roaring dragon

Drawing fantasy cartoon characters allows you to let your imagination run wild. Here you can learn how to draw a dragon by combining the features in these photographs. Try drawing more monstrous combinations using other animals.

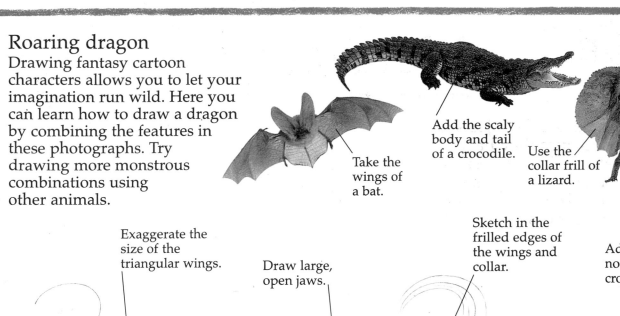

Take the wings of a bat.

Add the scaly body and tail of a crocodile.

Use the collar frill of a lizard.

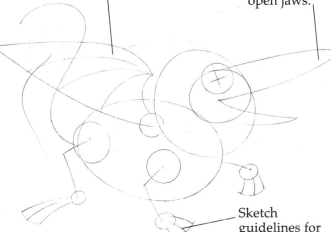

Exaggerate the size of the triangular wings.

Draw large, open jaws.

Sketch guidelines for the clawed feet.

1 Draw the basic body shapes, and tail and leg lines. Add ovals for the head and the frill of the lizard. Sketch in the wing shapes.

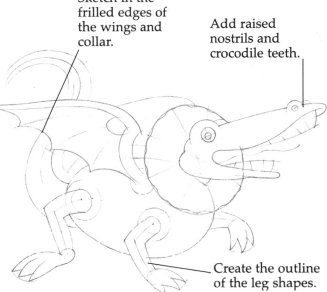

Sketch in the frilled edges of the wings and collar.

Add raised nostrils and crocodile teeth.

Create the outline of the leg shapes.

2 Fill in the outline of the basic body, head, and wing shapes. Add the eye and nostrils, and a large set of monstrous teeth.

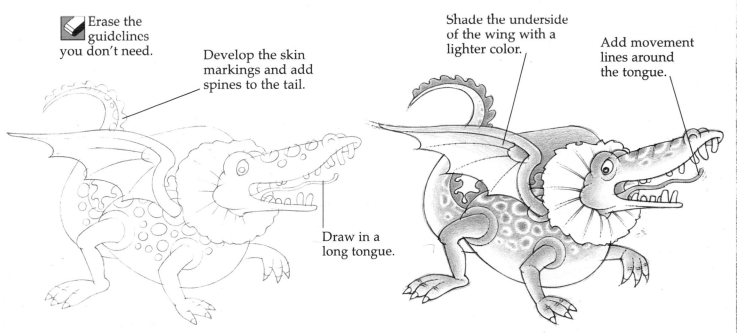

Erase the guidelines you don't need.

Develop the skin markings and add spines to the tail.

Draw in a long tongue.

Shade the underside of the wing with a lighter color.

Add movement lines around the tongue.

3 Spend time adding details, such as claws to the toes. Draw markings all over the body to give it a scaly look.

4 Finally, color in your roaring dragon, using bright green or any other color you imagine a dragon might be.

Adding human characteristics to your animal cartoons gives your drawings a whole new lease on life. On these pages, you can learn how to combine the features of an animal with the postures and movements of a human, with humorous results.

Use the body position of the girl.

Take the head of the rabbit.

Draw two long ovals for the rabbit's ears.

Draw a long curved line for the backbone.

Draw large sausage shapes for the feet.

The hands and nose begin as small circles.

Walking rabbit

Use these photographs to study the body shapes of the human being and the rabbit. Practice drawing the rough shapes first.

1 Draw shapes and guidelines for the rabbit's body, head, ears, nose, hands, feet, and tail. Add lines for the human legs and arms.

Erase the guidelines you don't need.

Add two large, square front teeth to a smiling mouth.

Color the underside of the ears pink.

Leave a hint of white in the nose.

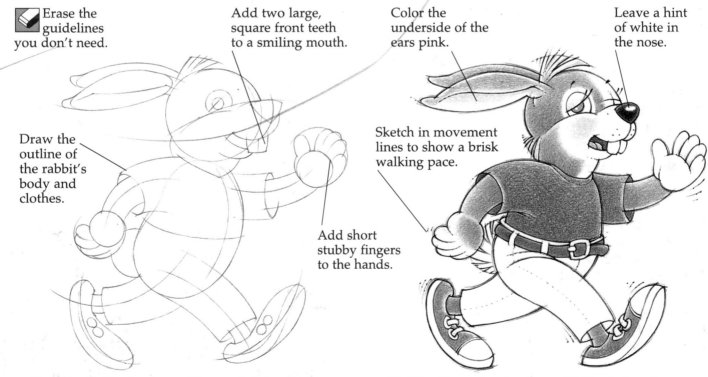

Draw the outline of the rabbit's body and clothes.

Sketch in movement lines to show a brisk walking pace.

Add short stubby fingers to the hands.

2 Sketch the body outline, adding clothes and shoes for a more human look. Use guidelines to create a spunky rabbit face.

3 Finally, color in the rabbit, giving it brightly colored clothes and shoes, some hair, and a glint in the eye.

Performing penguin

Here you can learn how to draw a trumpet-playing penguin. Use the photographs to help you combine the shapes of a penguin and a trumpet player.

The trumpet is made up of three ovals.

1 Draw the basic shapes of the penguin's body and head. Use guidelines to position the flippers like the trumpet player's arms.

The main body shape is a large oval.

Sketch in the large head and beak details.

Split the tail to make it look like a tuxedo jacket.

Complete the trumpet with a long cone shape.

2 Fill in the penguin outline, using the guidelines to position the details of the head and clothing.

Add a tuft of hair for a more human effect.

3 Finally, color in your cartoon. Add movement lines and music notes around the trumpet, to bring your character to life.

Movement lines animate the trumpet playing and foot tapping.

Skating elephant

Now try drawing an elephant roller skating! Exaggerate the size and shape of the elephant, to make it look funny in the unbalanced skating position.

1 Start by drawing the rough, circular guideline shapes of the elephant's body, head, and legs, positioned as the skater is in the photograph.

Draw short lines for arms and legs, with big ovals for the hands and feet.

Develop the outline shape of the face and head.

Add shape to the elephant's trunk.

2 Draw in the character outline, using guidelines to place the eye, ear, and trunk. Add clothes, helmet, skates, and knee and elbow pads.

Make the arms, legs, and body as chunky as possible.

3 Finally, color in the elephant, giving it brightly colored clothes and skates. Animate it with plenty of wobbly movement lines.

Movement lines along one side emphasize the lack of balance.

Cartoon faces

Here, you can learn how to draw expressive cartoon faces. Study the photographs on these pages and make different expressions in the mirror, too. You can then work out which are the best features to exaggerate to create the expression you want.

Happy face

Follow the steps on this page and draw a happy cartoon face based on this photograph of a smiling boy.

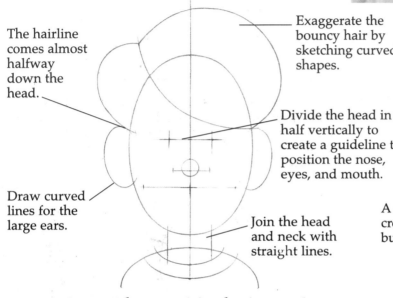

The hairline comes almost halfway down the head.

Exaggerate the bouncy hair by sketching curved shapes.

Divide the head in half vertically to create a guideline to position the nose, eyes, and mouth.

Draw curved lines for the large ears.

Join the head and neck with straight lines.

1 Start with an oval for the face and a half oval for the shoulders. Draw guidelines to position the facial features.

Start breaking up the hair to make it look voluminous.

Sketch tiny circles for the eyes.

A circle helps create a button nose.

Draw a wide crescent shape for the mouth.

2 As you sketch in the outlines of the facial features, remember to exaggerate them!

The large ears stick out noticeably.

Erase the guidelines you don't need.

Draw wavy lines for the hair.

Draw raised eyebrows.

A crooked, toothy smile makes the character look cute.

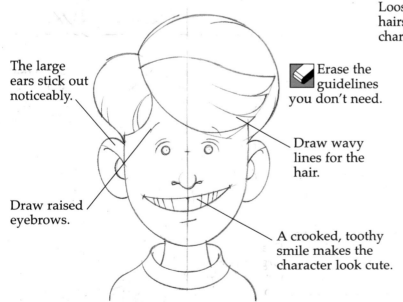

3 Spend time developing the mouth, eyes, and ears. Draw semicircles around the eyes to make them look young and bright.

Loose, wispy hairs give the character life.

Shade the face, leaving lighter areas for the teeth and around the eyes.

Take time to add the finishing touches to your character.

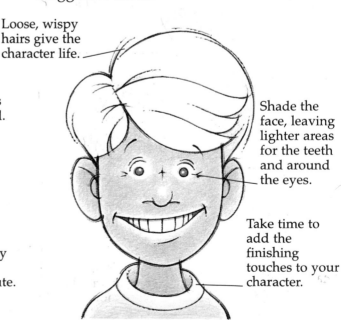

4 Color in your cartoon with bright colored pencils. Leave a glint of white in the eyes to make them sparkle.

Sad face

By lengthening all the features, you can make a face look sad.

The head is tilted slightly to one side.

Draw long, limp lines for the hair.

The chin is dropped down.

Sketch an elongated oval for the basic face shape.

Use guidelines to help you position the facial features.

Make a downturned curve for the mouth.

Curve small eyes and eyebrows downward.

Make the hair limp and wispy.

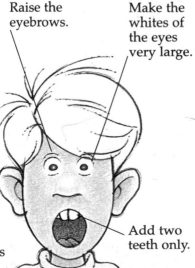

Angry face

An angry expression squashes the features together, narrowing the eyes and mouth.

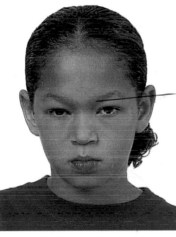

Draw basic shapes for the face and hair.

The eyes are narrowed and the eyebrows are angular.

Exaggerate the cheeks.

A middle part emphasizes the features bunching up in the center of the face.

Emphasize the V shape made by the eyebrows.

Use guides to sketch the eyes, nose, and mouth squashed up together.

Shade the face, leaving the eyes white and glaring.

Add lines around the eyes to emphasize the frown.

Surprised face

A surprised expression stretches the features apart and widens the eyes and mouth.

The chin is dropped and the nostrils are flared.

In a surprised expression, the eyes are above the line of the ears.

Make the hair spring up in the air.

Sketch an oval shape for the face.

Draw a large circle for the mouth.

Lift the shoulders for added emphasis.

Raise the eyebrows.

Make the whites of the eyes very large.

Add two teeth only.

Anyone can be an inspiration to draw a cartoon figure. The secret is to exaggerate body proportions and think of comical actions. These pages will teach you the basics. Once you have mastered the techniques, let your imagination run wild!

Sketch in a curved guideline down the middle of the body to help you draw the tilted pose.

Exaggerate the tilt in the body by drawing one shoulder higher than the other.

1 Draw simple oval shapes for the head, body, hands, and feet. Add long lines for the legs.

Make the bangs thick.

Draw flicked swinging ends to the hair.

Erase the guidelines you don't need.

Sketch in the fingers.

Draw shoelaces with large bows.

3 Complete the outline of the clothes and add a chunky belt.

Laughing girl
Use this photograph of a laughing girl to help draw an exaggerated cartoon character.

Use guidelines to add the small eyes and nose.

Draw a large semicircle for the laughing mouth.

Start to add the outline of the clothes.

Sketch in ovals for the fingers.

2 Sketch in the exaggerated body outline. Use guidelines to start building up the details of your cartoon.

The legs will look longer than they are in the photograph.

Leave the large teeth white.

Sketch in guidelines on the sneakers.

Shade the T-shirt in a bright color.

Ink in a dark outline around the cartoon.

4 Color in your laughing cartoon girl. Add laughter lines around her eyes.

Running boy

Here, you can learn how to draw a character sprinting fast. Use the photograph to help you decide which features to exaggerate.

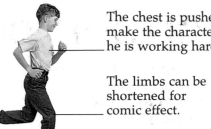

The chest is pushed out to make the character look as if he is working hard.

The limbs can be shortened for comic effect.

Movement lines add a feeling of speed.

Erase the guidelines you don't need.

Let the eyebrow show through the hair.

Add large drops of sweat.

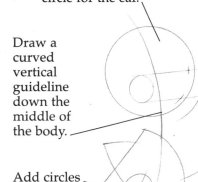

Sketch a large circle for the head and a smaller circle for the ear.

Draw a curved vertical guideline down the middle of the body.

Add circles for the hands.

Draw in a large mop of hair.

Use guidelines to position the facial features in profile.

Make the arms angular.

Red shading makes the face look hot.

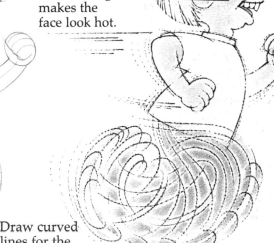

Draw curved lines for the feet positions.

1 Draw basic shapes and guidelines to help outline the figure. Sketch in a large oval for the running legs.

2 Sketch in the outlines of the clothes and face. Use guidelines to position the running leg lines.

3 Take time to draw in lines for the speedy legs. Finally, color in your cartoon.

Hands and fingers

Cartoon hands are bulkier than real hands. Practice drawing hands and fingers doing different things.

A simple circle forms the hand shape.

Draw short, stubby fingers, and circles for the nails.

Palm

Use unusual objects for comic effect.

Leave the fingernails white.

The fingers are elongated oval shapes.

Practice drawing hands holding or gripping objects.

1 Draw a basic circle, larger semicircle, and lines joining the two.

2 Use the basic shapes as a guide to sketch in the outline of the fingers.

3 Shade the hands to make them lifelike. Keep a dark outline.

Cartoon characters

Cartoons often play on stereotypes. They build on certain features and make them even more noticeable. Here you can see how to turn a girl into a giant. On the next page you will find step-by-step instructions on how to draw a baby and an eccentric old character.

Tall girl

Use a photograph of a girl and a cat as a point of reference and inspiration to help you draw your tall cartoon girl.

Draw a guideline down the middle of the girl's face.

The oval for the girl's head is almost as large as the oval for her body.

Sketch very long lines for the girl's arms and legs.

1 Draw ovals for the girl's head, body, hands, and feet. Break down the cat's shape into a series of oval shapes, too.

Use guidelines to position the girl's facial features.

Make the T-shirt sleeves short to emphasize the girl's long arms.

2 Sketch in the outline of the girl's long arms and legs, large head and feet, and small body. Start adding details to the cat.

Add a toy mouse for comic effect.

Erase the guidelines you don't need.

Sketch a large, mischievous grin.

Give the cat character by making it scowl.

Draw raised eyebrows and leave a glint of white in the eyes.

3 Complete the outlines of the girl, cat, and mouse. Add more details to build up the characters.

Short horizontal lines suggest the girl is patting the cat's head.

Large hands make the long arms seem even funnier.

4 Color in your cartoon girl, cat, and mouse. Take time to add finishing touches to the facial features.

Laughing baby girl

Use a picture of a girl and a young baby as a reference to help you draw a cute baby cartoon character.

Use the features of the girl's face, and the sitting position of the baby, to help you devise the cartoon character.

Draw a curved guideline down the center of the body.

Sketch a triangle for the baby's bangs.

Add a frilly bonnet.

One large tooth makes the mouth look larger and the character younger.

Leave a glint of white in the eyes.

A large block makes her fingers look smaller.

Use guidelines to add the facial features.

Add the outline of the clothes around the guidelines.

Draw tiny circles for the gripping fingers.

1 Draw basic shapes for the different parts of the body, and lines for the arms and legs.

2 Soften the outline shapes and start to add details on the face and clothes.

3 Use bright colors for your cartoon baby. Add chunky toys to emphasize her tiny size.

Eccentric old man

Use photographs of an old man to turn a young boy into an eccentric-looking cartoon character.

Use the man's body and the boy's smiling face to help you create your character.

Add glasses perched on the tip of the nose.

Add triangles for the hair on the balding head.

Draw an eccentric walking stick.

Make the hair wild and wispy.

Bundles of papers and books give a studious air.

Add a baggy sweater, large shirt collar, and over-long pants.

Use the guidelines to position the legs and arms.

Draw lines to show the pants creasing around the ankles.

1 Draw a large oval for the body and smaller ovals for the face, hands, and feet.

2 Firm up the outline shapes and start adding more details to the character.

3 Use a dark pencil or pen to draw a heavy outline and color in your cartoon.